IT'S ALL ABOUT TIGER

ON EVE OF OPEN, SOUTHERN HILLS ALIVE WITH TALK OF TAMING WOODS

CLASSIC GOLF

CLASSIC

INTRODUCTION BY RICK REILLY

THE PHOTOGRAPHS OF WALTER IOOSS JR

GOLF

HARRY N. ABRAMS, INC., PUBLISHERS

DON JANUARY, PGA Championship,

Columbine Country Club, Columbine Valley, Colorado, July 1967

GARY PLAYER, British Open, Royal Lytham & St. Annes Golf Club,

Lytham St. Annes, England, July 1974

ARNOLD PALMER AND JACK NICKLAUS,

Ligonier, Pennsylvania, July 1965

SIXTEENTH TEE, par 3, Cypress Point Golf Club,

Monterey, California, February 1979

CKNOWLEDGMENTS by Walter Iooss Jr

SPECTATORS, PGA Championship, Columbus Country Club, Columbus, Ohio, July 1964

NEWEST, LARGEST AND MOST
LUXURIOUS HOTEL IN MIAMI BEACH

Deauville

550 FT. ON THE OCEAN AT 67th STREET

600 incomparable guest rooms and suites • 2 pools • 2 night clubs • 3 dining rooms • ice skating rink • 18 hole championship golf course • complete shopping plaza • 100% air-conditioned.

Dear Dad,
Just arrived here today 3/19, Haven't been to beach yet and don't think I will. Never worked harder in my life. Whole Magazine depends on what I do. Am shooting Aaron, R. Penanowski, and Tony Lema, golfer. Am shooting Lema in color for Sport Mag Sunday. Should be home Wen. My room is 36.50 a nite. S.I. will kill me.
Love Walt

74608-B

Post Card

Mr Walter Iooss
50 Lefferts Ave
Brooklyn, N.Y.

AIR MAIL

8¢ U.S. AIR MAIL

WEST PALM BEACH MAR 20 PM 1964

IN NO SPORT ARE WE PHOTOGRAPHERS AS REVILED as in professional golf. Not only do the PGA officials not care for us, but often the fans despise us just as much. We're the lepers of the tour. I started to learn this on March 21, 1964, when I was assigned to photograph "Champagne" Tony Lema in Miami for *Sports Illustrated*. I was twenty years old and this was my first job covering golf. I knew nothing about the protocol a photographer was expected to follow to a tee, and little about the game of golf itself. Nor could I have been described as a "respecter of tradition," as Bert Yancy was in a 1960s PGA media guide. ¶ *A photographer must always stay as close to the gallery ropes as possible, and not stray onto the fairway to get a better angle.* I broke this rule-number-one when I first began covering Tony. I didn't do it purposely, I just hadn't been briefed on

the proper etiquette and never knew the rule existed. So, there I was in the middle of the fairway, caught like a deer in the headlights, when Tony started to lose it with me. He yelled and cursed, and then the gallery of Tony lovers turned on me. It was eighteen holes of humiliation.

Somehow I found out where Tony was staying and made an appointment to meet with him to apologize. I went to his hotel room and explained my ignorance. He accepted the apology, briefed me on the rules of the game, and we became friends.

On Sunday, July 24, 1966, I had just finished covering a PGA tournament in Akron, Ohio, and was bringing the film back to New York City on a chartered flight. *Sports Illustrated* always went to press on Sunday and there was no other way to get the film to the office in time.

I went to the men's room at the private airport and was standing at the urinal when "Champagne" Tony joined me at the adjacent fixture. I asked where has headed. He said to an exhibition in Chicago—his charter was leaving just before mine. We said goodbye. Within an hour, Tony's plane had crashed and he was dead. My friend was gone. I

had been one urinal away from death and didn't know it. So many charters I had traveled on to carry film back to the magazine, always on Sunday, often in horrible weather, and I thought many times that my clock was about to run out like Tony's had. I got so spooked that I asked S.I. to send someone else in my place. I had had enough and couldn't forget about Champagne.

If I never felt welcome on the courses, I came to appreciate and admire the pros, beginning with Palmer. Men loved him and woman adored him. My mother once said she wouldn't pass up a fling with Arnie—"he's so handsome and manly" (Mom was single at the time). Arnie always wore his heart on his tongue. He was a man of a thousand expressions as he swaggered about the links. No hat back then, no worries about the dangers of skin cancer; instead, a cavalier drag on a cigarette that fit the times— flicking it off the green just before a putt.

Then came Jack, plump and crew cut. He challenged Arnie's Army, became the enemy, and transformed himself into a swashbuckling, blond golf god. I spent a fair amount of time with Nicklaus. After years of shooting him in tournaments, I was hired by Hart, Schaffner & Marx, a clothier out of Chicago, to do a series of ads featuring Jack over a three-year period. The shoots were always done at his house or at the country club across the road. It was during these shoots that I became aware of the "bear stare." It appeared whenever Jack felt he was finished posing and wanted to move on.

On his property, he had two of the finest lawn tennis courts you would ever want to see. They were groomed like two huge putting greens. Jack said he planted different grasses on the courts to test for use on his golf courses. Back then I played tennis as often as I could. One day I arranged a doubles match on Jack's court, and he was one of my opponents. In the middle of the match, I was presented with a short lob at the net, one you could really get into. I saw Jack on the other side, and being a born competitor, I wanted to smash the ball close to him. I went for

it, and unfortunately I hit him—square in the back. That's when I saw the bear stare to end all bear stares.

In 1990, I was doing a series of photographs for *Sports Illustrated* called "Living Legends." You could argue that during that period some of the greatest athletes to ever represent their sports were active: Jordan, Magic, Moses, Carl Lewis, Gretzki, Connors, Ripken, and Jack.

I met him at the Loxahatchee Club in Jupiter, Florida, near his home. He brought a wardrobe to choose from and asked what I wanted to do: "You want to shoot a portrait?" Well, I had not planned to do a sitting portrait. In my mind, it was going to be an action shot. "No, it's not a portrait. I want to get you in your backswing just as you start to come down from the top."

"I can't do that because I just had a surgery to remove a cyst today," he answered.

"Can you fake it?"

(*left to right*) **WALTER IOOSS JR**, Spring Rock Country Club, Spring Valley, New York, June 1964; with the *Sports Illustrated* picture editor George Bloodgood, U.S. Open, Hazeltine National Golf Club, Chaska, Minnesota, May 1970; with photographer Tony Triolo, U.S. Open, May 1970. **APRIL MARCH, STRIPPER,** Spring Rock Country Club, Spring Valley, New York, June 1964 **DAN JENKINS** Doral Golf Resort, Miami, March 1976 **THE "A" TEAM**, Iooss, Jim Drake, and Neil Leifer, 1976

I'll try," and off we went. The background was a lake. The light on Jack was created with a four-by-eight foot mirror. Jack barely swung, but he did it well enough to create the shot on page 96. Jack could be accommodating if he wanted to.

The most amusing man I ever met in all of sports was Lee Trevino, but the last time I photographed him, he was doing something that I never thought could happen. He was in bed with his putter. I was shocked. It seemed like he had given up his life as a carouser for the sanctuary of his hotel room. His days of wine and women were over, and now he just wanted to regain his putting stroke.

Then there was Gary Player, the first golfer who worked at being physically fit—an exercise and health fanatic, he got the most out of his five-foot, seven-inch frame (page 136) and made the Arnie, Jack, and Lee show even more compelling. Player loved to wear all black during the summer tourneys, I think to show the other players he could take the heat.

On June 18, 2003, I followed Tiger Woods at the Buick Open and realized how incredible the pros really are. Tiger

resurrected golf from the ashes. Back in my golden era of Arnie, Jack, Lee, and Gary, when my own legs were young, I never much thought about the golfers' shot making, only my picture making. I confess that all of us photographers hoped the players would hook and slice themselves into terrible lies to create more dramatic shots. I covered thirty-seven tournaments for S.I. between 1964 and 1975. It seems odd how little I knew about how difficult a game it is to play. I played a bit back then, but quit in frustration. Maybe I did know, after all.

Back in my heyday of golf coverage, I had wonderful times with photographers and writers. Neil Leifer created an "A Team" that included himself; Jim Drake, the best golf photographer ever; and yours truly. The brilliant writer Dan Jenkins taught me nothing about golf but offered a master's degree in nightlife and cocktails. John Hanlon and Tony Triolo were amusing S.I. photographers to travel and work with.

I dedicate this book to my mother Barbara, my wife Eva, and my sons Christian and Bjorn.

Tiger Woods, World

"For every human who has ever lived there shines a star."
Arthur Clarke

Shot for NIKE in Orlando, Florida   May 2nd 2002

Greatest GOLFER...

...At the Windemere C.C. over 2 days from Dawn to noon. Lv for Charlotte

→ Scout for Earnhardt Jr.

INTRODUCTION by Rick Reilly

THE COOLEST GUY I EVER MET IN SPORTS was not Joe Namath, not Michael Jordan, not Tiger Woods. Wasn't a player or coach or even an owner. ¶ The all-time leader in cool—by a par 5—was Walter Iooss, photographer. ¶ I was twelve years old, a walking tube of Oxy 10, and more trouble than a BB gun. It was a fall Saturday in 1970, so I was doing what I always did on fall Saturdays in 1970—sneaking into a University of Colorado football game. You pretend you're in line to be a Coke vendor, then duck into the storage closet, through a window, out a door, hide with your feet on a toilet in a stall for an hour until the coast was clear and you're in! ¶ It was about two hours before kickoff when Walter saw me loitering in the stands, trying to look like I'd paid. He hollered up from the field, "Hey, kid, wanna make some easy money?"

Whoa. We didn't get Walter's kind in Boulder, Colorado, much then. We didn't get guys who looked like they'd just left Studio 54. He was Hollywood handsome, preposterously tan, stylishly long-haired, movie-star sunglasses. He looked like a guy who could date Angie Dickinson, have a Luger in the pocket of his trench coat, and speak Swahili, perhaps all at once.

I was over the wall and onto the field in seconds, all five feet, one inch and ninety pounds of me.

I dragged his cameras that day as he worked the sidelines—Colorado vs. Penn State—and he paid me twelve dollars. I'm sure I was overpaid at that. I was most probably useless, Frisbee-eyed at the cheerleaders, the players, the TV cameras, but mostly, him. I just stared at his clothes, his furious fingers, his *way*. My mind rollicked at the idea of *being* him—paid to be part of sports! Swimsuit shoots! Free shoe phones!

He moved smooth, talked smooth, *was* smooth. He whipped these big heavy cameras around like Bic pens. His motor drive was the coolest sound ever made. And when we got the cover of *Sports Illustrated*—five days

later—I use "we" here in the same way the guy who tapped Wilt Chamberlain's ankles says, "We scored 100 tonight"—I made getting a cool S.I. job my Number 1, no-doubt-about-it lifetime goal.

That's why I love this book. There's a coolness to these shots. If there's cool in a person, Walter tends to bring it out in film. Walter could make Erkl look cool. Walter never devoted himself to golf—Walter is probably too *cool* for golf, what with its plaid pants, country clubs just slightly more stuffy than Bea Arthur's underwear drawer, and human dandruffs in charge—and yet he found in the game a certain coolness like nobody before or since.

Take the way Walter shot Arnold Palmer. "There's never been anybody like Arnie to shoot," Walter says. "That swagger he had. So handsome. And he never wore a hat. Every photographer followed him. You couldn't stop looking at him!"

Like Tiger Woods now, you just couldn't go to a golf tournament in the 1960s and not follow Arnie. It was unthinkable, like getting your cotton candy during the Wallendas' act. And yet with all the thousands of shooters

JACK NICKLAUS, U.S. Open, The Olympic Club, San Francisco, June 1966

following Arnie over all those years, Walter has made some of the best pictures of him in history. Arnie with Eisenhower (page 38). (Who else but Arnie can jack with the President of the U.S.?) Arnie at Olympic (page 60). (Who else but Arnie can put fans in trees?) Arnie glaring at a shot (page 32). (Who else but Arnie can *shame* a ball into a hole?)

Pulled along in Arnie's Army, Walter saw things that would curl your putter. "I saw the Army move his ball, kick his ball, throw it back on the green," Walter remembers. "Of course it's illegal, but they'd do anything for their hero."

Arnie was easy to make look cool. Try doing it with Fat Jack.

When Jack Nicklaus stole Arnie's crown at the 1962 U.S. Open at Oakmount Country Club, he was a toll call from cool. Porky, butch haircut, the son of a pharmacist. But somehow, through those early years, Walter found the hidden Brad Pitt in Nicklaus waiting to come out. Check out Nicklaus on page 72, smoking a cigarette (he secretly smoked in those days), wearing Walter's glasses, his collar turned up. Somehow, Walter turned him into Fonzie.

Whaddya mean you're not givin' me that putt?

As he thinned, aged, and let his hair out, Nicklaus became more photogenic, but there may have never been a more heroic shot of The Golden Bear than Walter's British Open classic (page 76). Nicklaus peering stern-jawed over the top of a bunker. The wind in his tan face. His blond locks flowing back like Sampson visiting Scotland. If I'm Nicklaus, that's the one I ask them to use with my obit.

Like Nicklaus, Walter can dominate a room by walking into it, but he can also disappear like David Copperfield. Walter has this jewel-thief way about him. He can be quieter than a cat in socks. You can see that in so many of these pictures. My favorite in the book is Arnie and Jack

sitting in a clubhouse, 1965, Ligonier, Pennsylvania, just talking, a pack of Lark cigarettes on the table, some matches. Just two guys at the nineteenth hole, shooting the breeze, waiting for their beer. Is that Sam Snead in the background? Bob Rosburg? Billy Casper?

Except this particular photo is a swatch out of the royal cloth of golf—Jones to Hogan to Palmer to Nicklaus to Woods—and the brain boggles wondering what secrets The King is revealing to The Bear. Is he telling him to handle tempo? Bunker blasts? Women? You stare at it and stare at it. And you think, "How the *hell* did Walter get them to forget he was there?"

My two other Walter favorites, both spy jobs: Bob Hope and Bing Crosby, both trying to blend into the Pebble Beach fescue. Neither of them seemed to have the vaguest idea Walter existed, much less that he had a camera pointed at them. You know how you can tell? Neither is smiling. My Lord, Bob Hope would play to a Brownie with a Brownie if he thought it would get him some attention.

It wasn't just Walter's feet that were silent, it was his shutters. I dare you to look at any other golf photo book and see so many guys at the top of their golf swings. It's forbidden at a tournament to snap from the moment a player has stepped up to the ball to the time he's through impact. Better to walk up to the Queen and ask if she wants a bite of your corn dog. Pro golfers are just slightly more sensitive to sound than a sore-eared rabbit. A shutter clicking at the top sends most pros looking for murder, with a 3-iron to do their bidding. But look: Nicklaus at the top, Johnny Miller at the top, even Tiger Woods, whose ears were designed by the KGB, at the top. What's his secret?

"Man, I shoot and run!" Walter says. "Or I get so far away with a long lens that they can't hear. Or I play the wind. I get upwind of them so they can't hear the click. Or

I get in trees so if they hear me, at least they can't find me. Or I use a silencer. Or I hide in a big crowd." Of course, Walter probably leads the league in Tournaments Pitched Out Of. "Luckily, I could always find a way to talk my way back in."

One time, Walter nailed Bobby Nichols at impact on a putt and Nichols freaked. Why? Why is another question entirely. Kobe Bryant can shoot a free throw with 15,000 camera flashes going off at once but Bobby Nichols couldn't swing a driver when a shutter clicked fifty feet away. Anyway, the crowd—which happened to be many of Bobby's friends and family—turned on Walter the way the townspeople turn on Frankenstein. They came at him menacingly. All they lacked were torches and shovels. Walter bulled his chest.

"You wanna piece of me," Walter sneered, brandishing his bulky 300-millimeter lens like a billyclub, "you're gonna have to deal with this camera."

The camera saved Walter's butt. No wonder he Leica.

It used to be a form of entertainment among us ink-stained poets to watch a guy as cool as Walter get yelled at by the very uncool, self-important wool-covered globs who run most golf tournaments. It'd be like . . .

"Dandruff: Young man, I oughta throw the book at you! What you've done is a disservice to the time-honored game itself! Why, if Bobby Jones could see this . . .

Walter: Hey, man, if you want me to talk to this Bobby cat, I'll do it, OK? Just chill."

He hasn't changed much. The other day, he nailed Tiger at the top of his backswing, causing Woods' burly caddy/bouncer/goon Stevie Williams to stomp over to Walter and bark, "Ever cover a golf tournament before, mate?"

Maybe we oughta send Stevie this book.

I love the black and whites the best. As we all know,

black and whites give you more color than color. Like a man in bicycle shorts, it's hard to conceal the truth. Take the amazing shot of Chi Chi Rodriguez, fresh from Puerto Rico. For the love of Saltines, how skinny *was* Chi Chi then (page 100)? "I think I asked him once," Walter says. "His waist was twenty-eight inches." Check out the Ben Hogan (page 112). Walter seemed to find something almost *friendly* in Hogan. Hogan? Friendly? This is a man who was once approached by a young Johnny Miller, requesting to shake his hand. To which Hogan replied, "Hey, kid, can't you see I'm trying to eat my soup?"

There is something else I love about these shots—they're not about the golf, but the golfer.

Because Walter didn't play the game until these last few years, he didn't obsess over the golf shot itself, like so many shooters. He didn't really care to show just how hard the game is, how unthinkable it is that these guys can knock a little white wad of balata into an empty tuna can 473 yards away in three whacks when there are trees and water and sand and ice-cream carts in between. You won't see big-frame shots here designed to show the heroism of the shot. There's not a lot of jubilation stuff, crowds being amazed at what's just been done, players rejoicing at their luck or skill. The only thing close is a rare one of Lee Elder (page 188), the first black man ever to play in the Masters, celebrating a win.

The only thing close is anguish shots. Walter is very good at golf anguish shots. Of course, no sport doles out the anguish in heaping wheelbarrows full like golf. But honestly, do you not *love* Walter's shot of Tommy Nakajima's caddy burying his face in his hands as his man digs himself a grave in the famous Road Hole bunker at St. Andrews? When Nakajima rolled into that infamous bunker on the seventeenth hole during the 1978 British Open, he was near the lead. When he finally got out—five

shots later—he was in ruins. It was the single worst performance in the sand since the Republican Guard.

Do you not *ache* for Gary Player, also at St. Andrews on page 124, as he misses a putt on the eighteenth? But notice the frame of the shot. It's not just Player's agony, it's the entire *crowd's*.

But mostly what Walter gives you is the same great and rare skill that Annie Leibovitz gives you—a passion for faces. What you see is the *man*, who he is, what's written with the lines of his face, the fear or fury in his eyes. Look at Walter's gorgeous black and white of Lee Trevino on page 155. Trevino almost never shut up or settled down. He was a human espresso, fidgety and funny and frenzied. Once, on the first tee, Nicklaus turned to Trevino and said, "Now, I don't wanna do a lot of talking today, Lee."

And Trevino replied, "You don't have to do a lot of talking, Jack. You only gotta listen."

But Trevino was always golf's Pagliacci, always had laughter on the outside but more than his share of sorrow on the inside—his divorce, the ultimate loneliness he felt on the road, the racism he felt in his brown skin in a world where the balls, the flags, the power was all white. Somehow, Walter found this other, sad side of Trevino—without his family again, alone on Thanksgiving Day. You just never see Trevino like that: quiet and somber and *still*. It's like getting a jackrabbit to sit on your lap so you can pet it.

One of the best faces in the book belongs to the man who may have the best game of all—Woods. There's a particular bit of genius that I love—Walter convinced Woods to mimic his famous "shaded" look at his putting line (page 200). Tiger is so close, you feel like he's shading his way straight into your own eyes. And the thing that strikes you right away is that Tiger Woods must be one of the most allergic people ever to set foot on a golf course—the puffy lids, the swollen ducts, the runny nose. And he's the greatest outdoor pool shark in the world? Claritin has changed history.

Even rarer, if you follow golf, is the shot of Tiger hitting against some La Costa mansions (page 198). When's the last time you saw a shot of Tiger playing golf without a *single* other person in the frame? Do you know how hard that is? It's like getting a shot of Liza without a gimlet.

We all should thank Tiger, because Tiger has brought Walter back to the golf course. "Tiger is Arnie all over again," says Walter. "If he's not entered, it's a junior varsity tournament. He's the guy everybody wants to shoot and he's the only guy anybody wants to shoot. You can't take your eyes off him!"

Me, I've always made time to watch Walter.

By the way, I finally got that job I dreamed of—the S.I. job—fourteen years later. I've worked with Walter dozens of times, including the dreaded swimsuit shoot. Thirty-two years later, I still stare at him, amazed. But now I'm amazed at his preposterous skills, his charming lens-side manner, and his bottomless vat of energy. At sixty years old, Walter is still obsessed with taking lucky people like us into the soul of the people he shoots.

And that's *very* cool.

SPECTATORS, U.S. Open, Congressional Country Club, Bethesda, Maryland, June 1964

WINNIE PALMER, U.S. Open, Congressional Country Club, Bethesda, Maryland, June 1964

ARNOLD PALMER, PGA Championship, Laurel Valley Golf Club, Ligonier, Pennsylvania, July 1965

ARNOLD PALMER, Bing Crosby National Pro-Am, Pebble Beach Golf Links, Pebble Beach, California, January 1966

PALMER, PGA Championship, Laurel Valley Golf Club, Ligonier, Pennsylvania, July 1965

ARNOLD PALMER, U.S. Open, Congressional Country Club, Bethesda, Maryland, June 1964

DWIGHT EISENHOWER AND ARNOLD PALMER (*left*), Laurel Valley Golf Club, Ligonier, Pennsylvania, July 1965

PALMER AND MARK MCCORMICK, his powerful agent, Ligonier, Pennsylvania, July 1965

(*overleaf*) **PALMER,** PGA Championship, PGA National Golf Club, Palm Beach Gardens, Florida, February 1971

PALMER, U.S. Open, Congressional Country Club, Bethesda, Maryland, June 1964

ARNOLD PALMER (*above*), U.S. Open, Congressional Country Club, Bethesda, Maryland, June 1964

PALMER, Bing Crosby Pro-Am, Pebble Beach Golf Links, Pebble Beach, California, January 1966

ARNOLD PALMER, U.S. Open, Baltusrol Golf Club, Springfield, New Jersey, June 1967

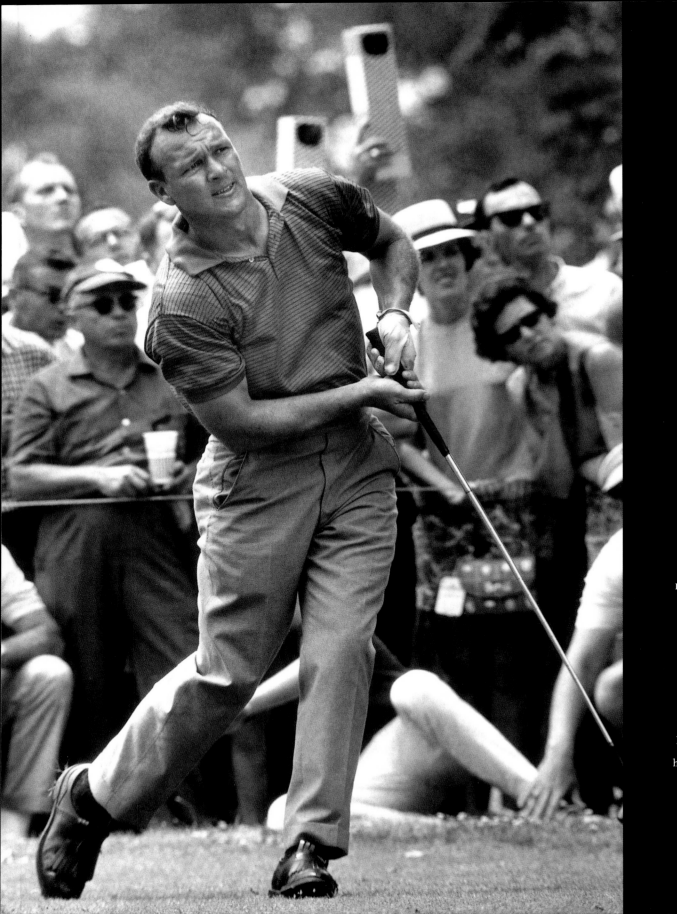

PALMER, U.S. Open, Baltusrol Golf
Club, Springfield, New Jersey,
June 1967

(*gatefold*) **PALMER,** U.S. Open,
The Olympic Club (Lake Course),
San Francisco, June 1966. Palmer
lost to Billy Casper in an eighteen-
hole playoff—Casper 67, Palmer 73.

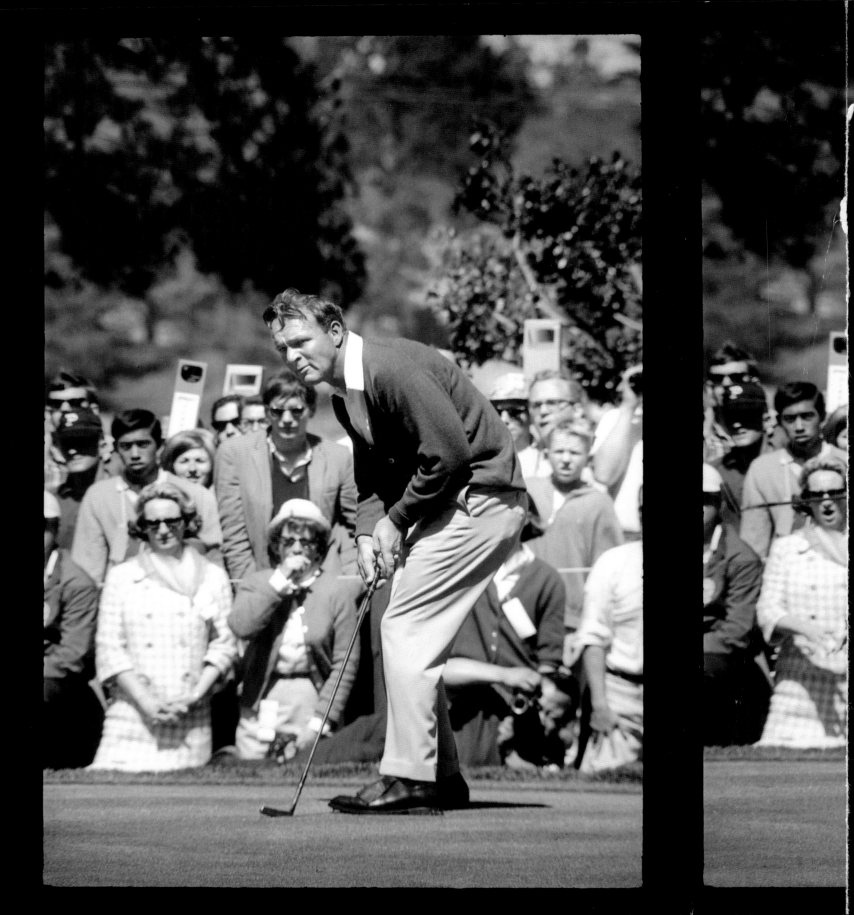

PALMER, Carling Open, Oakland Hills Country Club, Bloomfield Hills, Michigan, August 1964.

Palmer lost to Bobby Nichols by a single stroke.

BILLY CASPER AND ARNOLD PALMER tied in the final round,

U.S. Open, The Olympic Club, San Francisco, June 1966

ARNOLD PALMER, U.S. Open, Oakmount Country Club,

Oakmount, Pennsylvania, June 1973

PALMER preparing for U.S. Open, Hazeltine National Golf Club, Chaska, Minnesota, April 1970

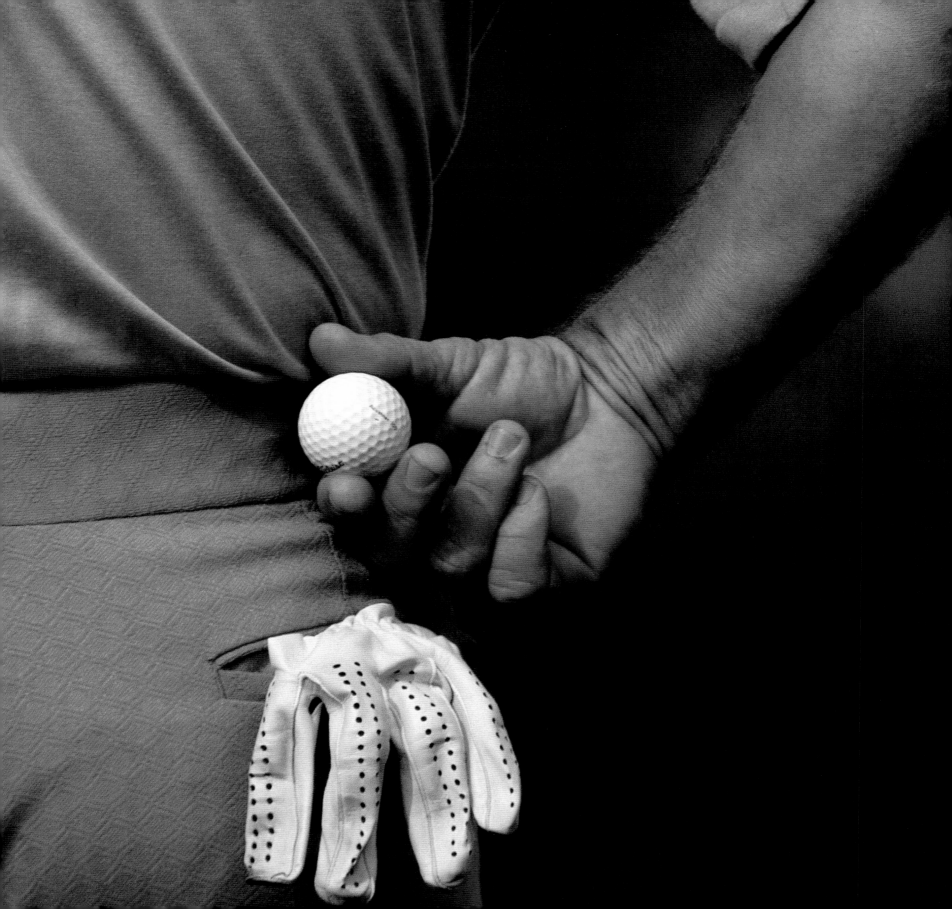

ARNOLD PALMER, U.S. Open, The Olympic Club,

San Francisco, June 1966

ARNIE, New York City, December 1999

THE SEVENTH HOLE, par 3, Bing Crosby Pro-Am, Pebble Beach

Golf Links, Pebble Beach, California, January 1966

PHIL ROGERS, U.S. Open, The Olympic Club, San Francisco, June 1966

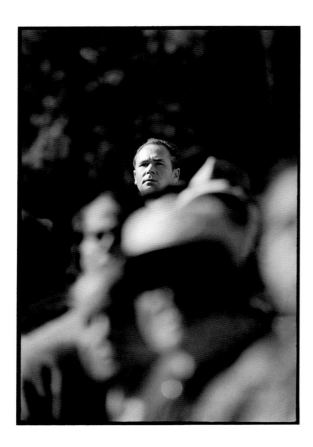

TONY LEMA, Bing Crosby Pro-Am, Pebble Beach Golf Links,

Pebble Beach, California, January 1966

SAM SNEAD, U.S. Open, Medinah Country Club (Number 3 Course),

Medinah, Illinois, June 1975

SAM SNEAD, PGA Championship, Firestone Country Club, Akron, Ohio, July 1966

NICKLAUS, U.S. Open, Bellerive Country Club, St. Louis, Missouri, June 1965

JACK NICKLAUS preparing for the U.S. Open, Hazeltine National Golf Club, Chaska, Minnesota, April 1970

JACK NICKLAUS (*left*), British Open, The Old Course at St. Andrews,
St. Andrews, Scotland, July 1978. Nicklaus won for the third time.
NICKLAUS, PGA Championship, PGA National Golf Club,
Palm Beach Gardens, Florida, February 1971

JACK NICKLAUS, PGA Championship, PGA National Golf Club, Palm Beach Gardens,

Florida, February 1971. This was Nicklaus's second PGA Championship win, making

him the first professional golfer to twice conquer the professional Grand Slam.

JACK NICKLAUS (*left*), PGA Championship, PGA National Golf Club, Palm Beach Gardens, Florida, February 1971

NICKLAUS, The Masters, Augusta National Golf Club, Augusta, Georgia, April 1977. Nicklaus needed to birdie the eighteenth hole in order
to tie Tom Watson for first, but he bogeyed it instead and lost the tournament by two strokes.

JACK NICKLAUS, PGA Championship, PGA National Golf Club, Palm Beach Gardens, Florida, February 1971

JACK, HAL SUTTON, AND JACK JR. (*from right to left*), U.S. Open, Merion Golf Club, Ardmore, Pennsylvania, June 1981

JACK NICKLAUS, U.S. Open, Baltusrol Golf Club, Springfield, New Jersey, June 1980.

He captured his fourth U.S. Open win.

JACK NICKLAUS (*left*) after winning his third Open title, British Open,

The Old Course at St. Andrews, St. Andrews, Scotland, July 1978

NICKLAUS, winning putt, U.S. Open, Baltusrol Golf Club,

Springfield, New Jersey, June 1980

NICKLAUS, PGA Championship, Firestone Country Club, Akron, Ohio, July 1966

NICKLAUS, The Masters, Augusta National Golf Club, Augusta, Georgia, April 1977

JACK NICKLAUS, U.S. Open, Pebble Beach Golf Links,

Pebble Beach, California, June 1972. He won his third Open title.

EIGHTEENTH HOLE OF DORAL GOLF RESORT, Miami, March 1976

JACK NICKLAUS (*clockwise, from top left*): PGA Championship, PGA National Golf Club, Palm Beach Gardens, Florida, January 1971; 75th U.S. Open, Medinah Country Club, Medinah, Illinois, June 1975; Preparing for the U.S. Open in Minnesota, April 1970; PGA Championship, PGA National Golf Club, Palm Beach Gardens, Florida, January 1971.
The Masters, Augusta National Golf Club, Augusta, Georgia, April 1977 (*opposite*)

JACK NICKLAUS, U.S. Open, Merion Golf Club, Ardmore, Pennsylvania, June 1981

NICKLAUS, U.S. Open, Oakmount Country Club, Oakmount, Pennsylvania, May 1973

(*overleaf*) **NICKLAUS,** Loxahatchee Club, Jupiter, Florida, 1990

JACK, New York City, December 1999

CHI CHI RODRIGUEZ (*left*), U.S. Open, Congressional Country Club, Bethesda, Maryland, June 1964

RODRIGUEZ, Carling Open, Oakland Hills Country Club, Bloomfield Hills, Michigan, August 1964

BING CROSBY at his Pro-Am, Pebble Beach Golf Links, Pebble Beach, California, January 1966

BOB HOPE, Bing Crosby Pro-Am, Pebble Beach, California, January 1966

GENE LITLER, PGA National Invitation, Colonial Country Club, Fort Worth, Texas, May 1964

TOM WEISKOPF, Jackie Gleason Inverrary-National Airlines Classic, Ft. Lauderdale, February 1973

TOMMY BOLT (*left*), PGA Championship, PGA National Golf Club, Palm Beach Gardens, Florida, February 1971

DAVID GRAHAM, U.S. Open, Merion Golf Club, Ardmore, Pennsylvania, June 1981

BEN HOGAN, U.S. Open, Baltusrol Golf Club, Springfield, New Jersey, June 1967

BEN HOGAN (*above*), PGA National Invitation, Colonial Country Club, Fort Worth, Texas, May 1964

HOGAN, Carling Open, Oakland Hills Country Club, Bloomfield Hills, Michigan, August 1964

BEN HOGAN, U.S. Open, Baltusrol Golf Club, Springfield, New Jersey, June 1967

KEN VENTURI after the final round, U.S. Open, Congessional Country Club, Bethesda, Maryland, June 1964.

Venturi won after being examined by a doctor for heat stroke thirty-six holes into the tournament. This was his only U.S. Open

VENTURI, U.S. Open, Congressional Country Club, Bethesda, Maryland, June 1964

BOBBY NICHOLS, Carling Open, Oakland Hills Country Club, Bloomfield Hills, Michigan, August 1964

TONY JACKLIN, U.S. Open, Hazeltine National Golf Club, Chaska, Minnesota, May 1970. Jacklin won.

GARY PLAYER, British Open, Royal Lytham & St. Annes Golf Club, Lytham St. Annes, England, July 1974. Player was forced to play this approach shot to the eighteenth green left handed, but did so successfully and claimed his third Open title. This win gave him the distinction of being one of two players ever that won an Open in three consecutive decades.

PLAYER WITH HIS CADDIE, RABBIT, British Open, Royal Lytham & St. Annes Golf Club, Lytham St. Annes, England, July 1974

GARY PLAYER, British Open, Royal Lytham & St. Annes Golf Club, Lytham St. Annes, England, July 1974

GARY PLAYER, British Open, Royal Lytham & St. Annes Golf Club, Lytham St. Annes, England, July 1974

GARY PLAYER, British Open, Royal Lytham & St. Annes Golf Club, Lytham St. Annes, England, July 1974

GARY PLAYER, U.S. Open, Bellerive Country Club, St. Louis, Missouri, June 1965.

He edged out Kel Nagle in an eighteen-hole playoff to win his only U.S. Open title—Player 71, Nagle 74.

PLAYER, PGA National Invitation, Colonial Country Club, Fort Worth, Texas, May 1964

GARY PLAYER with his family in Texas, April 1978

GARY PLAYER, U.S Open, Merion Golf Club,

Ardmore, Pennsylvania, May 1971

BILLY CASPER, U.S. Open, Baltusrol Golf Club, Springfield, New Jersey, June 1967

DOUG SANDERS, U.S. Open, The Olympic Club, San Francisco, June 1966

LEE TREVINO (*left*), PGA Championship, Tanglewood Golf Club, Clemmons, North

July 1974. Lee Trevino won supposedly using a putter he found in an attic.

TREVINO, U.S. Open, Oakmount Country Club, Oakmount, Pennsylvania, May

LEE TREVINO Byron Nelson Golf Classic, Preston Trail Golf Course, Dallas, May 1981

LEE TREVINO, U.S. Open, Merion Golf Club, Ardmore, Pennsylvania, June 1971. Trevino defeated Nicklaus in an eighteen-hole playoff for his second and last U.S. Open win— Trevino 68, Nicklaus 71.

LEE TREVINO (*above*), Byron Nelson Golf Classic, Preston Trail Golf Course, Dallas, May 1981

TREVINO, Bob Hope Desert Classic, Palm Springs, California, January 1979

LEE TREVINO, 10:15 P.M., Dallas hotel room, May 1981

LEE TREVINO as Pancho Villa, Tournament of Champions, Carlsbad, California, April 1969

LEE TREVINO (*above*), Tournament of Champions, Carlsbad, California, April 1969

TREVINO, El Paso, Texas, Thanksgiving Day 1972

LEE TREVINO (*left*), PGA Championship, Tanglewood Golf Club, Clemmons, North Carolina, July 1974. Trevino won.

TREVINO, Byron Nelson Golf Classic, Preston Trail Golf Course, Dallas, May 1981

(*overleaf*) **TREVINO,** U.S Open, Oak Hill Country Club, Rochester, New York, June 1968. Trevino won.

TREVINO'S

PAR 4 4 3 5 3 4 4
OUT 5 4 3 5 3 4 4

PAR 4 3 4 5 4 3 4
IN   4 2 3 5 4 3 4

Score	Hole		72	Par	443	534	44
en	71	Yancey			544	543	44
us	71	re no				3	44

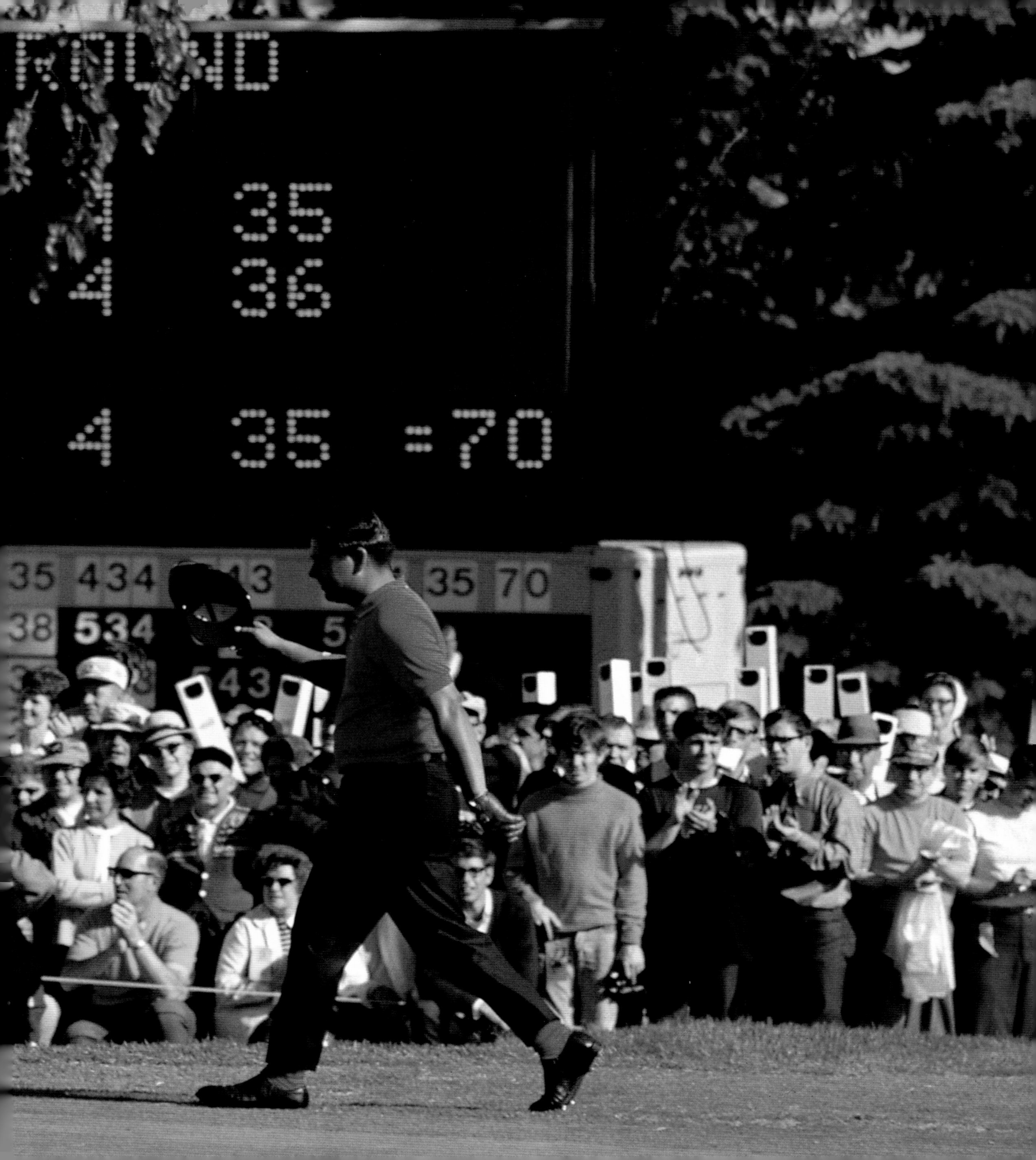

ROUND
35
4 36
4 35 =70
35 434 43 35 70
38 534
543

LEE TREVINO (*left*), Byron Nelson Golf Classic, Preston Trail Golf Course, Dallas, May 1981

TREVINO at home with his children, May 1981

LEE TREVINO (*left*), U.S. Open, Oakmount Country Club,

Oakmount, Pennsylvania, May 1973

TREVINO, World Cup of International Golf Association,

PGA National Golf Club, Palm Beach Gardens, Florida, November 1971

LEE TREVINO, January 1991

JOHNNY MILLER, British Open, Royal Lytham & St. Annes Golf Club,

Lytham St. Annes, England, July 1974

JOHNNY MILLER (*above*), U.S. Open, Oakmount Country Club, Oakmount, Pennsylvania, May 1973.

Miller shot a 63 in the final round, the lowest score ever shot in an Open tournament

at that time, and defeated John Schlee by a stroke.

MILLER, British Open, Royal Lytham & St. Annes Golf Club, Lytham St. Annes, England, July 1974

TOM WATSON (*left*), The Masters, Augusta National Golf Course, Augusta, Georgia, April 1978

WATSON, The Masters, Augusta National Golf Course, Augusta, Georgia, April 1977. Scoring a birdie on hole 17, Watson fired a final round 67 to beat Jack Nicklaus by two strokes.

TOM WATSON, U.S. Open, Baltusrol Golf Club, Springfield, New Jersey, June 1980

LEADERS
BURNS
GRAHAM D
VALENTINE
NICKLAUS
COOK
NORMAN
ROGERS
KRATZERT
WATSON

THRU 3
NORMAN

GREG NORMAN, U.S. Open, Merion Golf Club, Ardmore, Pennsylvania, June 1981

BEN CRENSHAW (*left*), U.S. Open, Atlanta Athletic Club, Duluth, Georgia, June 1976

CRENSHAW, U.S. Open, Medinah Country Club, Medinah, Illinois, June 1975

(*overleaf*) **CRENSHAW,** The Masters, Augusta National Golf Club, Augusta, Georgia, April 1977

CRENSHAW, Bing Crosby Pro-Am Golf Championships, Pebble Beach Golf Links, Pebble Beach, California, February 1979

SPECTATORS, British Open, St. Andrews Links, St. Andrews, Scotland, July 1978

CLUB PRO, Hanalei, Kauai, 1978

SEVE BALLESTEROS (*left*), U.S. Open, Baltusrol Golf Club, Springfield, New Jersey, June 1980

LANNY WADKINS, Glen Campbell LA Open, Riviera Country Club, Pacific Palisades, February 1975

THE MASTERS, Augusta National Golf Club, Augusta, Georgia, April 1977

TOMMY NAKAJIMA (*left*)**,** British Open, The Old Course at St. Andrews,

St. Andrews, Scotland, July 1978

ISAO AOKI, U.S. Open, Baltusrol Golf Club, Springfield, New Jersey, June 1980.

Aoki finished second, two strokes behind Jack Nicklaus.

THE MASTERS, Augusta National Golf Club,

Augusta, Georgia, April 1977

LEE ELDER WITH HIS WIFE, May 1975

CHARLIE SIFFORD, U.S. Open, Oak Hill Country Club,

Rochester, New York, June 1968

CADDIES, Vietnam Golf and Country Club, Ho Chi Minh City, Vietnam, August 2002

TIM HERRON AND TOM LEHMAN, Phoenix, January 2000

NICK PRICE, Orlando, November 1994

MARK O'MEARA (*left*), Orlando, November 1998

DAVIS LOVE III, Sea Island, Georgia, April 1999

(*overleaf*) **TIGER WOODS,** Orlando, May 2002

TIGER WOODS, La Costa Country Club,

Carlsbad, California, February 2000

TIGER WOODS (*left*), Orlando, March 2000

WOODS, La Costa Country Club, Carlsbad, California, February 2000

TIGER WOODS, Orlando, March 2000

TIGER WITH HIS AGENT, MARK STEINBERG, after his second U.S. Open victory,

Bethpage State Park, Farmingdale, New York, June 2002

(overleaf) **WOODS,** La Costa Country Club, Carlsbad, California, February 2000

WOODS, La Costa Country Club, Carlsbad,

California, February 2000

TIGER, New York City, December 2000

PROJECT MANAGER: Eric Himmel
EDITOR: Samantha Topol
DESIGNER: Michael J. Walsh Jr.
PRODUCTION MANAGER: Stanley Redfern

Library of Congress Cataloging-in-Publication Data

Iooss, Walter.
  Classic golf / photographs by Walter Iooss, Jr. ; introduction by Rick Reilly.
      p. cm.
Includes bibliographical references and index.
  ISBN 0-8109-4983-0
  1. Golf—Pictorial works. 2. Golfers—Portraits. I. Title.

  GV967.5.I66 2004
  796.352'022'2—dc22

                    2003025110

Photographs and preface copyright © 2004 Walter Iooss Jr.
Introduction © 2004 Rick Reilly

Printed and bound in China
10 9 8 7 6 5 4 3 2 1

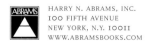

HARRY N. ABRAMS, INC.
100 FIFTH AVENUE
NEW YORK, N.Y. 10011
WWW.ABRAMSBOOKS.COM

ABRAMS IS A SUBSIDIARY OF

SPORTS Illustrated

Photo By	CREDIT	TAKE NO.
Walter Iooss Jr.		1

STORY & LOCATION Golf; $75,000 PGA National Golf Invitation at Colonial Country Club in Ft. Woth, Texas. 5/7/8/9	DEPT.

BLACK & WHITE FILM

35 mm	120	PACK	CUT	35 mm
9 10				

DEVELOPING & PRINTING INSTRUCTION

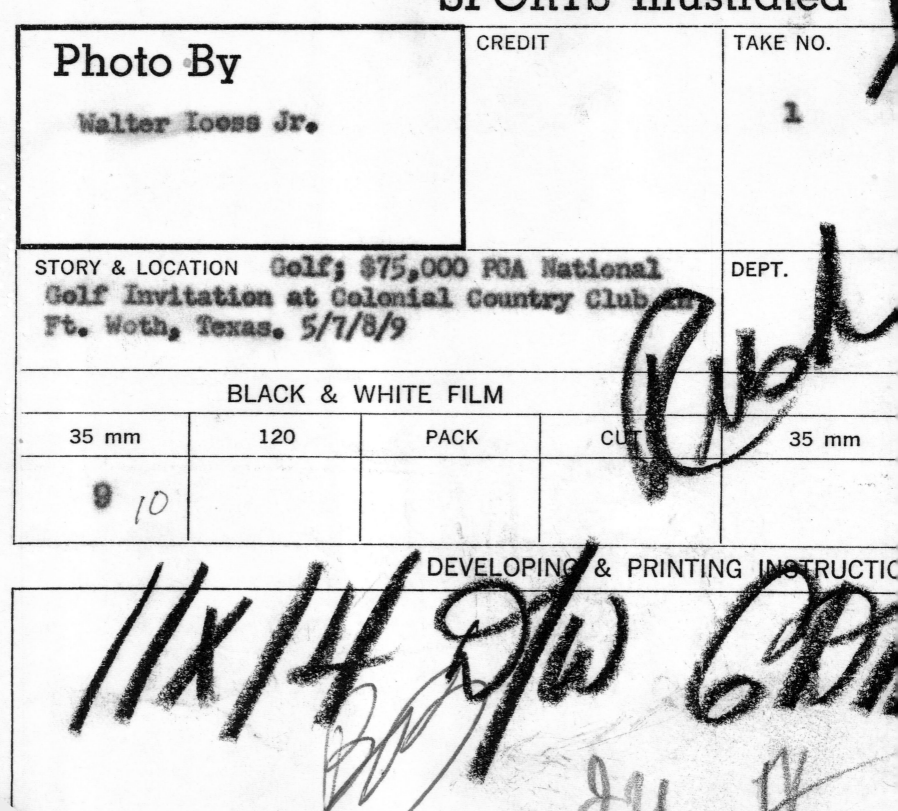

'ALS